A Leisure Arts Publication

VANNA'S CHOICE

Color it Beautiful Afghans

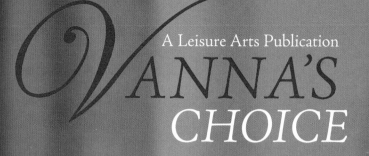

LEISURE ARTS, INC.
Little Rock, Arkansas

LION BRAND YARN COMPANY
New York, New York

EDITORIAL TEAM
Sandra Graham Case – Vice President & Editor-in-Chief
Cheryl Nodine Gunnells – Executive Publications Director
Susan White Sullivan – Senior Publications Director
Mark Hawkins – Senior Prepress Director
Debra Nettles – Designer Relations Director
Rhonda Shelby – Art Publications Director
Katherine Atchison – Photography Manager
Mary Sullivan Hutcheson – Technical Coordinator
Susan McManus Johnson – Associate Editor
Stephanie Johnson – Imaging Technician
Lora Puls – Senior Graphic Artist
Dayle Carozza – Graphic Artist
Amy Gerke – Graphic Artist
Becky Riddle – Publishing Systems Administrator
Clint Hanson – Publishing Systems Assistant
John Rose – Publishing Systems Assistant
Christy Myers – Lead Photography Stylist
Janna Laughlin – Photography Stylist
Lloyd Litsey – Staff Photograher
Mark Mathews & Ken West – Contributing Photographers

BUSINESS STAFF
Tom Siebenmorgen – Vice President & Chief Operations Officer
Pam Stebbins – Vice President of Sales & Marketing
Margaret Reinold – Sales and Service Director
Jim Dittrich – Vice President, Operations
Rob Thieme – Comptroller, Operations
Stan Raynor – Retail Customer Service Manager
Fred F. Pruss – Print Production Manager

LION BRAND PRODUCTION TEAM
Karen Tanaka – Creative Director
Jean Guirguis – Managing Editor
Jackie Smyth – Technical Editor
Liz Shaw – Design Editor
Merav Flam – Designer
Nadira Adams – Design Associate
Elizabeth Soper – Technical Associate

ISBN-13: 978-1-60140-685-9
ISBN-10: 1-60140-685-1

table of CONTENTS

a visit with **Vanna**

Just when I thought my favorite hobby couldn't get any better, I received a call from David Blumenthal, who had an exciting idea to share. David is the president and CEO of Lion Brand Yarn Company. I've worked with Lion Brand for years, helping to promote their products, so David knows that I'm Lion Brand's number one fan. He also knows how much I love to crochet, and he thought I would be interested in helping him develop a new product. And he was right! I've been looking forward to sharing David's idea with you ever since.

It's called Vanna's Choice, a premium yarn that's so very soft and luxurious! It's thrilling to have my name and image on the labels of this wonderful product. One of my favorite features of the yarn is the 23 colors that were chosen to work together beautifully. When colors blend this well, you know that whatever you crochet or knit will be lovely. And because Vanna's Choice is a premium acrylic yarn, it's washable. That's a nice convenience when you have a busy family like mine.

All these great qualities are enough to make anyone love crocheting with this yarn, but there is one more important thing that I want to be sure and mention: The Lion Brand Yarn Company supports St. Jude Children's Research Hospital, and so do I. You can rest assured that by using Vanna's Choice Yarn, you'll be buying a product from a company with integrity, a company that makes it a priority to give back to those in need. And St. Jude is the only pediatric research center where families never pay for treatment not covered by insurance. I'm fortunate to have two healthy children, Nicholas and Giovanna, but there are so many parents whose children desperately need the help they receive from St. Jude. It's the charity that's closest to my heart, so you know how excited I am to be a part of this endeavor.

Get involved! Have fun making afghans, scarves, hats, and slippers for your favorite charity. In Leisure Arts book *#4433 Vanna's Choice: Heartfelt Gifts to Knit and Crochet,* you'll find 25 patterns and lots of inspiration!

To show you the beauty of this new yarn, Lion Brand Yarn Company and Leisure Arts have teamed up to bring you this book, *Vanna's Choice: Color It Beautiful*. Several of the photos were taken in my home, so you can see the coordinating colors of Vanna's Choice in a real home environment. There are 15 cozy afghans to crochet, including a Warm Up America! pattern that you can use to create blankets for the popular charity or for your friends and family.

I often crochet on the set of Wheel of Fortune or while I'm traveling, and I enjoy the portability of projects made block-by-block. That's one reason why the 14 pattern stitches appeal to me. Also, by making the 10" blocks using the stitch pattern of your choice, you can make your own original afghans of any size or color. Try mixing the patterns and colors to create baby afghans, lap-size throws, or bed-size blankets. Starting on page 52, you'll see computer-generated images that will help you envision the afghans you can make with your own 10" blocks. It's fun to see how the pattern stitches give you a chance to be your own crochet designer.

So, take a look at these all-new patterns, choose your favorite shades of Vanna's Choice yarn, and see where your creativity takes you.

♡ *Vanna White*

YARN
information

From America's favorite crocheter, Vanna White, comes a specially designed yarn that is soft, washable, and available in a selection of colors that work together beautifully. Use Vanna's Choice yarn for everything from afghans to baby items and accessories—it's a perfect match for the lifestyle of today's busy family.

Linen .... #099

White .... #100

Pink .... #101

Navy .... #110

Beige .... #123

Taupe .... #125

Rust .... #135

Dusty Rose .... #140

Rose .... #142

Silver Blue .... #105

Dusty Blue .... #108

Colonial Blue .... #109

Chocolate .... #126

Honey .... #130

Brick .... #133

Antique Rose .... #143

Dusty Purple .... #146

Purple .... #147

Black .... #153

Mustard .... #158

Pea Green .... #170

Dusty Green .... #173

Olive .... #174

Of course you're familiar with the Granny Square. With its fast and simple repetitions of three double crochets, it's been a popular crochet block for years. But have you ever thought about all the ways you can expand on the pattern? In fact, expanding a Granny Square block is how you create this colorful baby blanket. After completing three rounds of the first color, you then alternate colors with each successive round and keep going until your afghan is the size you want. For this baby blanket, a 36" square is perfect.

—Vanna

baby BLANKET

EASY

Finished Size: 36" x 36" (91.5 x 91.5 cm)

MATERIALS
LION BRAND® Vanna's Choice Worsted Weight
    yarn [3½ ounces, 170 yards
    (100 grams, 156 meters) per ball]
    1 ball #170 Pea Green (A)
    1 ball #142 Rose (B)
    2 balls #105 Silver Blue (C)
    2 balls #135 Rust (D)
    2 balls #108 Dusty Blue (E)
    2 balls #125 Taupe (F)
    or colors of your choice
LION BRAND crochet hook size J-10 [6 mm]
    or size needed for gauge
LION BRAND large-eyed blunt needle

GAUGE
11 dc-groups + 7 rnds = 4" [10 cm]
BE SURE TO CHECK YOUR GAUGE.

COLOR SEQUENCE
Work 2 rnds with A, *1 rnd with A, 1 rnd with B, 1 rnd with C, 1 rnd with D, 1 rnd with E, 1 rnd with F; rep from * for Color Sequence.

BLANKET
With A, ch 4; join with sl st in first ch to form a ring.

Rnd 1: Ch 3 (counts as first dc here and throughout), 2 dc in ring, *ch 1, 3 dc in ring; rep from * 2 more times, ch 1; join with sl st in top of beg-ch.

Rnd 2: Sl st in first ch-1 sp, ch 3, (2 dc, ch 1, 3 dc) in same sp (first corner dc-group made), *(3 dc, ch 1, 3 dc) in next ch-1 sp (corner dc-group made); rep from * 2 more times; join with sl st in top of beg-ch.

Rnd 3: Sl st in first ch-1 sp, ch 3, (2 dc, ch 1, 3 dc) in same ch-1 sp, *3 dc in sp between next 2 dc-groups, (3 dc, ch 1, 3 dc) in next ch-1 sp; rep from * 2 more times, 3 dc in sp between next 2 dc-groups; join with sl st in top of beg-ch. Fasten off.

Rnd 4: Join next color of Color Sequence with a sl st in any corner ch-1 sp, ch 3, (2 dc, ch 1, 3 dc) in same ch-1 sp, *(3 dc in sp between next 2 dc-groups) to next ch-1 sp, (3 dc, ch 1, 3 dc) in next ch-1 sp; rep from * 2 more times, (3 dc in sp between next 2 dc-groups) to beg-ch; join with sl st in top of beg-ch. Fasten off.

Rnds 5-32: Continue in Color Sequence; join next color with sl st in any ch-1 sp; rep Rnd 4, increasing 1 dc-group each side every rnd.

Fasten off.

FINISHING
Weave in ends.

My grandmother, Albertene Nicholas, would have loved the look of this toasty afghan. The heathered appearance comes from holding together one strand each of two different-color yarns, and the afghan works up quickly using a large hook. Like the Baby Blanket, it's really just a very large Granny Square block.

—Vanna

great AFGHAN

Finished Size:
62" x 62" (157.5 x 157.5 cm)

MATERIALS
LION BRAND® Vanna's Choice
  Worsted Weight yarn
  [3½ ounces, 170
  yards (100 grams, 156 meters)
  per ball]
  10 balls #123 Beige (A)
  10 balls #125 Taupe (B)
  or colors of your choice
LION BRAND crochet hook size
  N-13 [9 mm] or size needed
  for gauge
LION BRAND large-eyed blunt
  needle

GAUGE
Rnds 1-3 of square = 3" [7.5 cm]
with 1 strand each of A and B
held together.
BE SURE TO CHECK YOUR
GAUGE.

NOTE: Afghan is worked with 1 strand each of A and B held together throughout.

AFGHAN
With 1 strand each of A and B held tog, ch 4; join with sl st in beg ch to form a ring.

Rnd 1: Ch 3 (counts as first dc here and throughout), 2 dc in ring, ch 2, (3 dc in ring, ch 2) 3 times; join with sl st in top of beg ch-3.

Rnd 2: Sl st to first ch-2 sp, ch 3, 2 dc in same sp, ch 2, 3 dc in same sp, ch 1, *(3 dc, ch 2, 3 dc) in next ch-2 sp, ch 1; rep from * 2 more times; join with sl st in top of beg ch-3.

Rnd 3: Sl st to ch-2 sp, ch 3, 2 dc in same sp, ch 2, 3 dc in same sp, ch 1, 3 dc in next ch-1 sp, ch 1, *(3 dc, ch 2, 3 dc) in next ch-2 sp, ch 1, 3 dc in next ch-1 sp, ch 1; rep from * 2 more times; join with sl st in top of beg ch-3.

Rnd 4: Sl st to ch-2 sp, ch 3, 2 dc in same sp, ch 2, 3 dc in same sp, ch 1, (3 dc in next ch-1 sp, ch 1) to next ch-2 sp, *(3 dc, ch 2, 3 dc) in next ch-2 sp, ch 1, (3 dc in next ch-1 sp, ch 1) to next ch-2 sp; rep from * 2 more times; join with sl st in top of beg ch-3.

Continue as established, working (3 dc in next ch-1 sp, ch 1) 1 more time each side every rnd until piece measures 62" x 62" (157.5 x 157.5 cm). Fasten off.

FINISHING
Weave in ends.

Isn't this little throw restful in shades of blue and linen? It's a good size for when you just need extra warmth on your legs and feet. I also think this afghan would be sweet for a baby boy. Try your own selections of Vanna's Choice yarn to see how this design would look in different hues. On page 18, you can see how colors can change the 'mood' of your design.

—Vanna

lapBLANKET

■■□□ **EASY**

Finished Size: 36" x 36" (91.5 x 91.5 cm)

MATERIALS

LION BRAND® Vanna's Choice Worsted Weight yarn [3½ ounces, 170 yards (100 grams, 156 meters) per ball]
    2 balls #099 Linen (A)
    2 balls #105 Silver Blue (B)
    2 balls #108 Dusty Blue (C)
    or colors of your choice
LION BRAND crochet hook size J-10 [6 mm] or size needed for gauge
LION BRAND large-eyed blunt needle

GAUGE

11 dc-groups + 7 rnds = 4" [10 cm]
BE SURE TO CHECK YOUR GAUGE.

COLOR SEQUENCE

* Work 1 rnd with A, 1 rnd with B, 1 rnd with C; rep from * for Color Sequence.

BLANKET

With A, ch 4; join with sl st in first ch to form a ring.

Rnd 1: Ch 3 (counts as first dc here and throughout), 2 dc in ring, *ch 1, 3 dc in ring; rep from * 2 more times, ch 1; join with sl st in top of beg-ch. Fasten off.

Rnd 2: Join next color of Color Sequence with a sl st in any corner ch-1 sp, ch 3, (2 dc, ch 1, 3 dc) in same sp (first corner dc-group made), *(3 dc, ch 1, 3 dc) in next ch-1 sp (corner dc-group made); rep from * 2 more times; join with sl st in top of beg-ch. Fasten off.

Rnd 3: Join next color of Color Sequence with a sl st in any corner ch-1 sp, ch 3, (2 dc, ch 1, 3 dc) in same ch-1 sp, *3 dc in sp between next 2 dc-groups, (3 dc, ch 1, 3 dc) in next ch-1 sp; rep from * 2 more times, 3 dc in sp between next 2 dc-groups; join with sl st in top of beg-ch. Fasten off.

Rnd 4: Join next color of Color Sequence with a sl st in any corner ch-1 sp, ch 3, (2 dc, ch 1, 3 dc) in same ch-1 sp, *(3 dc in sp between next 2 dc-groups) to next ch-1 sp, (3 dc, ch 1, 3 dc) in next ch-1 sp; rep from * 2 more times, (3 dc in sp between next 2 dc-groups) to beg-ch; join with sl st in top of beg-ch. Fasten off.

Rnds 5-30: Continue in Color Sequence; join next color with sl st in any ch-1 sp; rep Rnd 4, increasing 1 dc-group each side every rnd. At end of Rnd 30, do not fasten off.

FINISHING
Border
Ch 4, (dc, ch 1) 5 times in ch-2 sp, sc in next ch-1 sp, *ch 1, (dc, ch 1) 4 times in next ch-1 sp, sc in next ch-1 sp, rep from * around working (dc, ch 1) 6 times in corner ch-2 spaces. Fasten off. Weave in ends.

two-tone
AFGHAN

◼◼◻◻ EASY

Finished Size: 62" x 62" (157.5 x 157.5 cm)

MATERIALS

LION BRAND® Vanna's Choice Worsted Weight
  yarn [3½ ounces, 170 yards
  (100 grams, 156 meters) per ball]
  8 balls #108 Dusty Blue (A)
  8 balls #125 Taupe (B)
  or colors of your choice
LION BRAND crochet hook size J-10 [6 mm]
  or size needed for gauge
LION BRAND large-eyed blunt needle

GAUGE

Rnds 1-3 of square = 2" [5 cm]
BE SURE TO CHECK YOUR GAUGE.

NOTE: To keep Afghan square, join each new color
  in a different corner of each round.

COLOR SEQUENCE

*Work 1 rnd A, 1 rnd B; rep from * for Color Sequence.

AFGHAN

With A, ch 4; join with sl st in beg ch to form a ring.

Rnd 1: Ch 3 (counts as first dc here and throughout), 2 dc in ring, ch 2, (3 dc in ring, ch 2) 3 times; join with sl st in top of beg ch-3. Fasten off.

Rnd 2: Join B with sl st in any ch-2 sp, ch 3, 2 dc in same sp, ch 2, 3 dc in same sp, ch 1, *(3 dc, ch 2, 3 dc in next ch-2 sp) 3 times, ch 1; rep from * 2 more times; join with sl st in top of beg ch-3. Fasten off.

Rnd 3: Join A with sl st in any corner ch-2 sp, ch 3, 2 dc in same sp, ch 2, 3 dc in same sp, ch 1, 3 dc in next ch-1 sp, ch 1, *(3 dc, ch 2, 3 dc) in next ch-2 sp, ch 1, 3 dc in next ch-1 sp, ch 1; rep from * 2 more times; join with sl st in top of beg ch-3. Fasten off.

Rnd 4: Join next color of Color Sequence with sl st in any corner ch-2 sp, ch 3, 2 dc in same sp, ch 2, 3 dc in same sp, ch 1, (3 dc in next ch-1 sp, ch 1) to next ch-2 sp, ch 1, *(3 dc, ch 2, 3 dc) in next ch-2 sp, ch 1, (3 dc in next ch-1 sp, ch 1) to next ch-2 sp; rep from * 2 more times; join with sl st in top of beg ch-3. Fasten off.

Continue as established, working (3 dc in next ch-1 sp, ch 1) one more time each side every rnd until piece measures 62" [157.5 cm] square.

FINISHING
Weave in ends.

Have you noticed how popular brown and aqua have been lately? This afghan will look perfect in a room decorated with similar colors. And yes, I do carry a big project bag with me almost everywhere so I can keep my crochet close at hand.

—Vanna

17

Here are those color examples I promised. They show how the Granny Square puts on a new personality with every color change. Feeling bold? Try making a square in each different color of Vanna's Choice yarn until you have enough for an afghan.

—Vanna

multi-colorSQUARE

■■□□ EASY

Finished Size: 10" x 10" (25.5 x 25.5 cm)

MATERIALS
LION BRAND® Vanna's Choice Worsted Weight yarn [3½ ounces, 170 yards (100 grams, 156 meters) per ball]
1 ball #099 Linen (A)
1 ball #173 Dusty Green (B)
1 ball #170 Pea Green (C)
1 ball #174 Olive (D)
or colors of your choice
LION BRAND crochet hook size K-10.5 (6.5 mm) or size needed for gauge
LION BRAND large-eyed blunt needle

NOTE: Materials are sufficient to make 5 squares.

GAUGE
17 dc + 7 rnds = 4" (10 cm)
BE SURE TO CHECK YOUR GAUGE.

COLOR SEQUENCE
*Work 1 rnd with A, 1 rnd with B, 1 rnd with C, 1 rnd with D; rep from * for Color Sequence.

GRANNY SQUARE

With A, ch 4. Join with sl st to form a ring.

Rnd 1: Ch 3, 2 dc in ring (counts as first dc here and throughout), *ch 2, 3 dc in ring, rep from * 3 times, ch 2, sl st into top of beg ch to join. Fasten off A.

Rnd 2: Join B with sl st in any ch-2 sp, ch 3 (2 dc, ch 2, 3 dc) in same sp, *ch 1, (3 dc, ch 2, 3 dc) in next ch-2 sp, rep from * ch 1, end with sl st into top of beg ch. Fasten off B.

Rnd 3: Join C with sl st in any ch-2 sp, ch 3 (2 dc, ch 2, 3 dc) in same sp , *ch 1, 3 dc in next ch-1 sp, ch 1, (3 dc, ch 2, 3 dc) in next ch-2 sp, rep from * ch 1, end with sl st into top of beg ch. Fasten off C.

Rep Rnd 3, changing colors as in Color Sequence, and inc 1 dc group each side every round for 8 rounds total, end with D. Fasten off.

FINISHING
Weave in ends.

alternate COLORS

LION BRAND® Vanna's Choice Worsted Weight
yarn [3½ ounces, 170 yards (100 grams, 156 meters) per ball]
1 ball #102 Dusty Rose (A)
1 ball #146 Dusty Purple (B)
1 ball #142 Rose (C)
1 ball #147 Purple (D)
or colors of your choice

LION BRAND® Vanna's Choice Worsted Weight
yarn [3½ ounces, 170 yards (100 grams, 156 meters) per ball]
1 ball #135 Rust (A)
1 ball #133 Brick (B)
1 ball #130 Honey (C)
1 ball #126 Chocolate (D)
or colors of your choice

log cabin
AFGHANS

The Log Cabin pattern is inspired by a popular quilt block, and it's another classic block design that can just keep growing until you have a finished afghan. I especially like patterns that don't take your full attention the entire time you are crocheting—once you've established the center and the first four sides, you can simply keep going. And here's another benefit of the large single block—there's no need to join lots of little blocks!

—Vanna

babyBLANKET

NOTE: To change color work last stitch of first color until 2 loops remain on hook, yarn over with next color, draw yarn through 2 loops on hook. Turning chain does not count as stitch.

EASY +

Finished Size: 36" x 36" (91.5 x 91.5 cm)

MATERIALS

Lion Brand® Vanna's Choice Worsted Weight yarn [3½ ounces, 170 yards (100 grams, 156 meters) per ball]
MEDIUM 4
1 ball #170 Pea Green (A)
2 balls #140 Dusty Rose (B)
2 balls #135 Rust (C)
2 balls #099 Linen (D)
1 ball #143 Antique Rose (E)
1 ball #125 Taupe (F)
or colors of your choice
Lion Brand crochet hook size I-9 [5.5 mm] or size needed for gauge
Lion Brand large-eyed blunt needle

GAUGE

11 hdc + 10 rows = 4" [10 cm]
BE SURE TO CHECK YOUR GAUGE.

COLOR SEQUENCE

Center square in A, *3 rows B, 3 rows C, 3 rows D, 3 rows E, 3 rows D, 3 rows B, 3 rows A, 3 rows C, 3 rows F, 3 rows D, 3 rows B, 3 rows A; repeat from * for Color Sequence.

AFGHAN
Center Square

With A, ch 10.

Row 1: Hdc in 3rd ch from hook and in each ch across – 8 hdc.

Rows 2-6: Ch 2, turn, hdc in each hdc across; change to B in last st of Row 6.

First Strip

Row 1: With B, turn piece clockwise 90 degrees to work along ends of rows of Center Square, ch 2, work 8 hdc evenly spaced across ends of rows of Center Square – 8 hdc.

Rows 2 and 3: Ch 2, turn, hdc in each hdc across; change to C in last st of Row 3.

Second Strip

Row 1: With C, turn piece clockwise 90 degrees to begin work along ends of rows of First Strip, ch 2, work 4 hdc evenly spaced across ends of rows of First Strip; working in opposite side of foundation ch of Center Square, hdc in each ch across – 12 hdc.

Rows 2 and 3: Ch 2, turn, hdc in each hdc across; change to D in last st of Row 3.

Third Strip

Row 1: With D, turn piece clockwise 90 degrees to begin work along ends of rows of Second Strip, ch 2, work 4 hdc evenly spaced across ends of rows of Second Strip, work 8 hdc evenly spaced across ends of rows of Center Square – 12 hdc.

Rows 2 and 3: Ch 2, turn, hdc in each hdc across; change to E in last st of Row 3.

Fourth Strip

Row 1: With E, turn piece clockwise 90 degrees to begin work along ends of rows of Third Strip, ch 2, work 4 hdc evenly spaced across ends of rows of Third Strip, hdc in each hdc across center section, work 4 hdc evenly spaced across ends of rows of previous strip – 16 hdc.

Rows 2 and 3: Ch 2, turn, hdc in each st across; change to D in last st of Row 3.

Next Strip

Row 1: Turn piece clockwise 90 degrees to begin work along ends of rows of strip just completed, ch 2, work 4 hdc evenly spaced across ends of rows of strip just completed, hdc in each hdc across center strip, then work 4 hdc evenly spaced across ends of rows of previous strip.

Rows 2 and 3: Ch 2, turn, hdc in each hdc across; change to next color in Color Sequence in last st of Row 3.

Rep Rows 1 – 3 of Next Strip to work new strips in Color Sequence until work measures 36" x 36" [91.5 x 91.5 cm]. Fasten off.

FINISHING

Weave in ends.

lapAFGHAN

EASY +

Finished Size: 36" x 36" (91.5 x 91.5 cm)

MATERIALS

LION BRAND® Vanna's Choice Worsted Weight
yarn [3½ ounces, 170 yards
(100 grams, 156 meters) per ball]
2 balls #125 Taupe (A)
2 balls #110 Navy (B)
2 balls #099 Linen (C)
2 balls #174 Olive (D)
or colors of your choice
LION BRAND Size N-13 [9 mm] crochet hook
or size needed for gauge
LION BRAND large-eyed blunt needle

ALTERNATE COLORS

LION BRAND® Vanna's Choice Worsted Weight
yarn [3½ ounces, 170 yards
(100 grams, 156 meters) per ball]
2 balls #146 Dusty Purple (A)
2 balls #143 Antique Rose (B)
2 balls #142 Rose (C)
2 balls #140 Dusty Rose (D)
or colors of your choice

GAUGE

11 hdc and 8 rows = 4" [10 cm]
BE SURE TO CHECK YOUR GAUGE.

COLOR SEQUENCE

Center square in A, *3 rows B, 3 rows C, 3 rows D,
3 rows A; rep from * for Color Sequence.

NOTE: To change color, work last stitch until there are 3 loops on hook, yarn over with new color and draw through all loops on hook to complete stitch.

AFGHAN
Center Square
With A, ch 10.

Row 1: Hdc in 3rd ch from hook and in each ch across – 8 hdc.

Rows 2-6: Ch 2, turn, hdc in each hdc across; change to B in last st of Row 6.

First Strip
Row 1: With B, turn piece clockwise 90 degrees to work along ends of rows of Center Square, ch 2, work 8 hdc evenly spaced across ends of rows of Center Square – 8 hdc.

Rows 2 and 3: Ch 2, turn, hdc in each hdc across; change to C in last st of Row 3.

Second Strip
Row 1: With C, turn piece clockwise 90 degrees to begin work along ends of rows of First Strip, ch 2, work 4 hdc evenly spaced across ends of rows of First Strip; working in opposite side of foundation ch of Center Square, hdc in each ch across – 12 hdc.

Rows 2 and 3: Ch 2, turn, hdc in each hdc across; change to D in last st of Row 3.

Third Strip
Row 1: With D, turn piece clockwise 90 degrees to begin work along ends of rows of Second Strip, ch 2, work 4 hdc evenly spaced across ends of rows of Second Strip, work 8 hdc evenly spaced across ends of rows of Center Square – 12 hdc.

Rows 2 and 3: Ch 2, turn, hdc in each hdc across; change to A in last st of Row 3.

Fourth Strip

Row 1: With A, turn piece clockwise 90 degrees to begin work along ends of rows of Third Strip, ch 2, work 4 hdc evenly spaced across ends of rows of Third Strip, hdc in each hdc across center section, work 4 hdc evenly spaced across ends of rows of previous strip – 16 hdc.

Rows 2 and 3: Ch 2, turn, hdc in each st across; change to B in last st of Row 3.

Next Strip

Row 1: Turn piece clockwise 90 degrees to begin work along ends of rows of strip just completed, ch 2, work 4 hdc evenly spaced across ends of rows of strip just completed, hdc in each hdc across center strip, then work 4 hdc evenly spaced across ends of rows of previous strip.

Rows 2 and 3: Ch 2, turn, hdc in each hdc across; change to next color in Color Sequence in last st of Row 3.

Rep Rows 1-3 of Next Strip to work new strips in Color Sequence until work measures 36" x 36" (91.5 x 91.5 cm). Fasten off.

FINISHING
Edging

Join B with sl st anywhere along outside edge of Afghan. Work 1 round hdc evenly spaced around Afghan, working 3 hdc at each corner; join with slip st in top of first hdc. Fasten off.

Weave in ends.

Just look how much Nicholas and Giovanna have grown since my last crochet book! I can hardly believe it. Doesn't Giovanna look cozy under that pink-and-purple afghan? Nicholas' afghan is handsome in earthy shades. Each afghan is a single Log Cabin block. Stacking the colors, instead of staggering them around the center, changes the design completely.

—Vanna

ripple
AFGHANS

It's easy to see that family time is important at our house. We're snugglers, whatever the season, so it's nice to have a few afghans handy. The ripple pattern for afghans has been around a long time, but isn't it amazing what yarn color can do to refresh a classic design?

—Vanna

This kilim rug-inspired afghan was an instant hit when Lion Brand announced the release of Vanna's Choice yarn. It uses almost all of the yarn colors, and they blend exceptionally well. I think using colors that are made to work together is the key to a design's success.

—Vanna

kilimTHROW

◼◼◻◻ EASY

Finished Size: 48" x 66" (122 x 167.5 cm)

MATERIALS
LION BRAND® Vanna's Choice Worsted Weight yarn [3½ ounces, 170 yards (100 grams, 156 meters) per ball]
MEDIUM 4
3 balls #125 Taupe (A)
3 balls #123 Beige (B)
3 balls #130 Honey (C)
3 balls #140 Dusty Rose (D)
2 balls #133 Brick (E)
2 balls #108 Dusty Blue (F)
2 balls #158 Mustard (G)
2 balls #170 Pea Green (H)
2 balls #143 Antique Rose (J)
2 balls #173 Dusty Green (K)
1 ball #126 Chocolate (L)
1 ball #174 Olive (M)
1 ball #146 Dusty Purple (N)
1 ball #105 Silver Blue (O)
1 ball #099 Linen (P)
1 ball #147 Purple (Q)
1 ball #109 Colonial Blue (R)
1 ball #110 Navy (S)
1 ball #135 Rust (T)
or colors of your choice
LION BRAND Size P-15 [10 mm] crochet hook or size needed for gauge
LION BRAND large-eyed blunt needle

GAUGE
13 sts and 8 rows = 5" [12.5 cm] in pattern stitch with 2 strands of yarn held together.
BE SURE TO CHECK YOUR GAUGE.

STITCH EXPLANATION
sc2tog (sc decrease): Insert hook into st and draw up a loop. Insert hook into next st and draw up a loop. Yarn over, draw through all 3 loops on hook.

NOTES: 1) Afghan is worked with 2 strands held together throughout and following Color Sequence. 2) To change color work last stitch of first color until 2 loops remain on hook, yarn over with next color, draw yarn through 2 loops on hook to complete stitch.

COLOR SEQUENCE
Work 3 rows of each of the following color combinations:
* 1 strand each of A and B,
1 strand each of D and E,
1 strand each of C and M,
1 strand each of J and L,
1 strand each of C and K,
1 strand each of B and J,
1 strand each of D and G,
1 strand each of N and O,
1 strand each of C and P *,
1 strand each of E and G,
1 strand each of A and K,
1 strand each of H and Q,
1 strand each of F and T,
1 strand each of A and R,
1 strand each of D and E,
1 strand each of H and S,
1 strand each of C and D;
rep from * to * once, then work 3 rows with 1 strand each of A and B held tog.

AFGHAN

With Color 1 (1 strand each of A and B held tog), ch 118.

Row 1 (WS): Sc in 2nd ch from hook and next 5 ch, 3 sc in next ch, *sc in next 5 ch, sk next 2 ch, sc in next 5 ch, 3 sc in next ch; rep from *, ending sc in last 6 ch – 9 "ripples". Fasten off.

Row 2 (WS): Do not turn, join Color 1 yarn with sl st in first sc; working in back loops only, ch 1, sc2tog, sc in next 5 sc, 3 sc in next sc, *sc in next 5 sc, sk next 2 sc, sc in next 5 sc, 3 sc in next sc; rep from * across, ending sc in next 5 sc, sc2tog.

Row 3 (RS): Ch 1, turn; working in both loops, sc2tog, sc in next 5 sc, 3 sc in next sc, *sc in next 5 sc, sk next 2 sc, sc in next 5 sc, 3 sc in next sc; rep from * across, ending sc in next 5 sc, sc2tog. Fasten off Color 1.

Row 4 (RS): Using Color 2 (1 strand each of D and E held tog), work as for Row 2.

Rows 5 and 6: Work as for Row 3, changing to Color 3 at end of Row 6.

Rows 7-9: Work as for Row 3. Fasten off Color 3 at end of Row 9.

Row 10 (WS): Using Color 4, work as for Row 2.

Rows 11 and 12: Work as for Row 3, changing to Color 5 at end of Row 12.

Continue to rep Rows 7-12, following Color Sequence and working 3 rows in each color. Complete entire Color Sequence twice, then work 3 rows with Color 1. Do not fasten off Color 1.

FINISHING
Edging

Row 1: With Color 1, sc evenly across long side of afghan.

Rows 2 and 3: Ch 1, turn, sc in each sc across.

Fasten off. Rep Edging on opposite long side of afghan.

Weave in ends.

I usually choose traditional pastels for baby blankets—you know, pink, blue, green, yellow— but the soft shadings in this blanket work just as well for an infant as they do for an adult.

—Vanna

shadedBLANKET

◗◗■□□ **EASY**

Finished Sizes
Baby Afghan: 26" x 27½" (66 x 70 cm)
Adult Afghan: 38" x 44" (96.5 x 112 cm)

NOTE: Pattern is written for Baby Afghan with changes for Adult Afghan in parentheses. When only one number is given, it applies to both sizes. To follow pattern more easily, circle all numbers pertaining to your size before beginning.

MATERIALS
LION BRAND® Vanna's Choice Worsted Weight yarn [3½ ounces, 170 yards (100 grams, 156 meters) per ball]
2 (3) balls #170 Pea Green (A)
1 (2) balls #130 Honey (B)
1 (2) balls #143 Antique Rose (C)
1 (2) balls #133 Brick (D)
1 (2) balls #135 Rust (E)
or colors of your choice
LION BRAND crochet hook size J-10 [6 mm] or size needed for gauge
LION BRAND large-eyed blunt needle

GAUGE
17 sts + 9½ rows = 4" [10 cm] in ripple pattern
BE SURE TO CHECK YOUR GAUGE.

STITCH EXPLANATION
sc2tog (sc decrease): Insert hook into stitch and draw up a loop. Insert hook into next stitch and draw up a loop. Yarn over, draw through all 3 loops on hook.

COLOR SEQUENCE
*Work 4 rows with A, 4 rows with B, 4 rows with C, 4 rows with D, 4 rows with E; rep from * for Color Sequence.

NOTE: To change color, work last stitch until 2 loops remain on hook, yarn over with new color, and draw yarn through 2 loops on hook to complete stitch.

AFGHAN
With A, ch 101 (152).

Row 1: Sc in 2nd ch from hook and next 6 ch, 3 sc in next ch, *sc in next 7 ch, sk next 2 ch, sc in next 7 ch, 3 sc in next ch; rep from *, ending sc in last 7 ch – 6 (9) "ripples".

Row 2: Ch 1, turn, sc2tog, sc in next 6 sc, 3 sc in next sc, *sc in next 7 sc, sk next 2 sc, sc in next 7 sc, 3 sc in next sc; rep from * across, ending sc in next 6 sc, sc2tog.

Rep Row 2, changing colors following Color Sequence for a total of 60 (100 rows).

Last 4 Rows: With A, rep Row 2 four times.

Fasten off.

FINISHING
Left Side Edging
From RS, join A at top of left side.

Row 1: With A, working in ends of rows, sc evenly spaced along straight edge of afghan.

Rows 2-4: Ch 1, turn, sc in each sc across.
Fasten off.

Right Side Edging
From RS, join B at lower corner of right side. Work as for Left Side Edging.

Weave in ends.

tassledAFGHAN

■■□□ **EASY**

Finished Size: 48" x 60" (122 x 152.5 cm)

MATERIALS
LION BRAND® Vanna's Choice Worsted
  Weight yarn [3½ ounces,
  170 yards (100 grams, 156
  meters) per ball]
  4 balls #135 Rust (A)
  3 balls #125 Taupe (B)
  3 balls #133 Brick (C)
  3 balls #130 Honey (D)
  3 balls #126 Chocolate (E)
  or colors of your choice
LION BRAND Size K-10.5 [6.5 mm] crochet
  hook or size needed for gauge
LION BRAND large-eyed blunt needle

GAUGE
12 sts and 4½ rows = 4" [10 cm] in ripple
pattern
BE SURE TO CHECK YOUR GAUGE.

STITCH EXPLANATION
dc3tog (dc decrease 2 sts): Yarn over, insert
hook into stitch and draw up a loop, yarn over
and draw through 2 loops. [Yarn over, insert
hook into next stitch and draw up a loop. Yarn
over, draw through 2 loops] twice, yarn over
and draw through all loops on hook.

COLOR SEQUENCE
*Work 2 rows with A, 2 rows with B, 2 rows
with C, 2 rows with D, 2 rows with E; rep from
* for Color Sequence.

NOTE: To change color, work last
stitch until 2 loops remain on hook,
yarn over with new color and draw
yarn through loops on hook to
complete stitch.

AFGHAN
With A, ch 176.

Row 1: Dc in 3rd ch from hook and
next 7 ch, (3 dc in next ch) twice, *dc
in next 7 ch, (dc3tog) twice, dc in
next 7 ch, (3 dc in next ch) twice; rep
from * across to last 10 ch, dc in next
7 ch, dc3tog – 8 ripples.

Row 2: Ch 2, turn, dc3tog, dc in each
of next 7 dc, (3 dc in next dc) twice,
*dc in each of next 7 dc, (dc3tog)
twice, dc in each of next 7 dc, (3 dc
in next dc) twice; rep from * across
to last 10 dc, dc in next 7 dc, dc3tog;
change to B in last st.

Rows 3 and 4: Rep Row 2 for ripple
pattern; change to C in last st.

Continue to rep Rows 3 and 4,
following Color Sequence. Complete
entire Color Sequence seven times
then work 2 more rows with A, for a
total of 72 rows. Fasten off.

FINISHING
Fringe
Cut 170 strands of A, each 14" (35.5
cm) long. For each fringe, hold 10
strands together and fold in half. Use
crochet hook to draw fold through
Afghan, forming a loop. Pull ends
of fringe through this loop. Pull to
tighten. Make fringe on every 'point'
along both ends of Afghan.
Weave in ends.

When I look at this afghan, I can almost feel the cooling air of autumn in South Carolina, where I grew up. These rich colors give the afghan real presence, and the tassels add a touch of luxury.

—Vanna

Nicholas is beyond the age of playing with toy dinosaurs, but there certainly was a time when he could recite their Latin names. The combination of blue, green, and taupe would make this afghan a good gift for anyone who loves any aspect of nature—or natural history.

—Vanna

lapTHROW

🔴🔴⬜⬜ EASY

Finished Size: 36" x 37" (91.5 x 94 cm)

MATERIALS

LION BRAND® Vanna's Choice Worsted Weight yarn [3½ ounces, 170 yards (100 grams, 156 meters) per ball] **MEDIUM 4**
2 balls #109 Colonial Blue (A)
2 balls #170 Pea Green (B)
2 balls #110 Navy (C)
2 balls #125 Taupe (D)
2 balls #099 Linen (E)
or colors of your choice
LION BRAND Size N-13 [9 mm] crochet hook or size needed for gauge
LION BRAND large-eyed blunt needle

GAUGE

14 stitches and 10 rows = 4" [10 cm] in ripple pattern
BE SURE TO CHECK TO YOUR GAUGE.

STITCH EXPLANATION

sc2tog (sc decrease): Insert hook into stitch and draw up a loop. Insert hook into next stitch and draw up a loop. Yarn over, draw through all 3 loops on hook.

COLOR SEQUENCE

*Work 4 rows with A, 4 rows with B, 4 rows with C, 4 rows with D, 4 rows with E; rep from * for Color Sequence.

NOTE: To change color, work last stitch until 2 loops remain on hook, yarn over with new color and draw yarn through loops on hook to complete stitch.

AFGHAN

With A, ch 134.

Row 1: Beginning in 2nd ch from hook, sc2tog, sc in next 7 ch, 3 sc in next ch, *sc in next 8 ch, sk next 2 ch, sc in next 8 ch, 3 sc in next ch; rep from * to last 9 ch, sc in next 7 ch, sc2tog in last 2 ch – 7 ripples.

Row 2: Ch 1, turn, sc2tog, sc in next 7 sc, 3 sc in next sc, *sc in next 8 sc, sk next 2 sc, sc in next 8 sc, 3 sc in next sc; rep from * across to last 9 sc, sc in next 7 sc, sc2tog.

Row 3 and 4: Rep Row 2 for ripple pattern; change to B in last st.

Rows 5 - 8: Rep Row 2; change to C in last st of Row 8.

Continue to rep Rows 5-8, following Color Sequence. Complete entire Color Sequence four times and work 4 more rows with A, for a total of 84 rows. Fasten off.

FINISHING
Edging

Join C in any st along edge of Afghan. Work sc evenly spaced around edge of Afghan; join with slip st in first sc. Fasten off. Weave in ends.

33

striped AFGHANS

Of all the crochet patterns there are, a striped design has to be one of the easiest to do. That makes it perfect for design-as-you-go projects. The color combinations can be as limited or varied as you choose, and never be afraid to experiment with color! For instance, did you ever think that shades of brown and tan could feel festive? When I wrapped this throw around my shoulders, it reminded me of a serape in desert hues. I could almost hear a Spanish guitar playing.

—Vanna

neutralAFGHAN

●□□□ BEGINNER

Finished Size: 48" x 65" (122 x 165 cm)

MATERIALS
LION BRAND® Vanna's Choice Worsted Weight
yarn [3¹/₂ ounces, 170 yards
(100 grams, 156 meters) per ball]
4 balls #126 Chocolate (A)
4 balls #099 Linen (B)
3 balls #125 Taupe (C)
4 balls #123 Beige (D)
or colors of your choice
LION BRAND Size N-13 [9 mm] crochet hook or
size needed for gauge
LION BRAND large-eyed blunt needle

GAUGE
11 double crochet and 8 rows = 4" [10 cm]
BE SURE TO CHECK YOUR GAUGE.

NOTE: To change color, work last stitch of first color until 2 loops remain on hook, yarn over with next color, draw yarn through 2 loops on hook to complete stitch.

AFGHAN
With A, chain 135.

Row 1: Double crochet in 4th chain from hook and in each chain across; change to B in last stitch —- 132 double crochet.

Row 2: Chain 3, turn, double crochet in each double crochet across; change to C in last stitch.

Row 3: Chain 1, turn, single crochet in each double crochet across; change to D in last stitch.

Row 4: Chain 1, turn, single crochet in each single crochet across.

Row 5: Chain 3, turn, double crochet in each single crochet across; change to A in last stitch.

Row 6: Chain 1, turn, single crochet in each double crochet across; change to B in last stitch.

Row 7: Chain 3, turn, double crochet in each single crochet across; change to C in last stitch.

Row 8: Chain 3, turn, double crochet in each double crochet across; change to D in last stitch.

Row 9: Chain 3, turn, double crochet in each double crochet across; change to A in last stitch.

Row 10: Chain 1, turn, single crochet in each double crochet across.

Row 11: Chain 3, turn, double crochet in each single crochet across; change to B in last stitch.

Repeat Rows 2 through 11 eleven more times, then repeat Rows 2 through 10, for a total of 130 rows. Fasten off.

FINISHING
Weave in ends.

Did I say Spanish guitar? Nicholas does like to entertain us with foot-tapping songs, but they're usually more along the line of rock 'n' roll. In keeping with the tempo, the quick-to-crochet lap robe is a combination of lively Vanna's Choice colors worked while holding two strands together.

—Vanna

multi-colorAFGHAN

Finished Size:
48" x 57" (122 x 145 cm)

MATERIALS
LION BRAND® Vanna's Choice Worsted Weight yarn [3½ ounces, 170 yards (100 grams, 156 meters) per ball]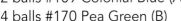
2 balls #109 Colonial Blue (A)
4 balls #170 Pea Green (B)
3 balls #123 Beige (C)
3 balls #133 Brick (D)
3 balls #126 Chocolate (E)
or colors of your choice
LION BRAND Size P-15 [10 mm] crochet hook or size needed for gauge
LION BRAND large-eyed blunt needle

GAUGE
7 double crochet and 4½ rows = 4" [10 cm] with 2 strands of yarn held together.
BE SURE TO CHECK YOUR GAUGE.

NOTES: 1) Afghan is worked with 2 strands of yarn held together throughout. 2) To change color, work last stitch of first colors until 2 loops remain on hook, yarn over with next colors, draw yarn through 2 loops on hook to complete stitch.

AFGHAN
With 1 strand each of A and B held together, chain 86.

Row 1: Double crochet in 3rd chain from hook and in each chain across —- 84 double crochet.

Row 2: Chain 3, turn, double crochet in next double crochet and each double crochet across, ending with double crochet in top of turning chain; change to 1 strand each of B and C in last stitch. Fasten off A.

Rows 3 and 4: Chain 3, turn, double crochet in next double crochet and each double crochet across, ending with double crochet in top of turning chain;

change to 1 strand each of C and D in last stitch of Row 4. Fasten off B.

Rows 5 and 6: Work as for Row 3, changing to 1 strand each of D and E in last stitch of Row 6. Fasten off C.

Rows 7 and 8: Work as for Row 3, changing to 1 strand each of B and E in last stitch of Row 8. Fasten off D.

Rows 9 and 10: Work as for Row 3, changing to 1 strand each of A and B in last stitch of Row 10. Fasten off E.

Rows 11 and 12: Work as for Row 3, changing to 1 strand each of B and C in last stitch of Row 12. Fasten off A.

Repeat Rows 3 through 12 five more times, for a total of 62 rows. Fasten off.

FINISHING
Weave in ends.

This afghan looks like it was made for Giovanna! The shades of dusty rose, brick, and honey are almost as sweet as she is. I do love to crochet for my friends and family. It's a wonderfully relaxing hobby that helps to make my work hours fly until I can get home to my children. I'm glad that you've also discovered the fun of crochet. And I hope you will always have plenty of time in your life for both creativity and family.

—Vanna

tweedLAP AFGHAN

◼◼◻◻ EASY

Finished Size: 36" x 36" (91.5 x 91.5 cm)

MATERIALS

LION BRAND® Vanna's Choice Worsted Weight
yarn [3½ ounces, 170 yards
(100 grams, 156 meters) per ball]

MEDIUM 4

3 balls #133 Brick (A)
3 balls #140 Dusty Rose (B)
3 balls #130 Honey (C)
or colors of your choice
LION BRAND crochet hook size P-15 [10 mm] or
size needed for gauge
LION BRAND large-eyed blunt needle

GAUGE

7½ dc + 4 rows = 4" [10 cm] with 2 strands of yarn held together.
BE SURE TO CHECK YOUR GAUGE.

COLOR SEQUENCE

*Work 2 rows with one strand each of A and B held together, work 2 rows with one strand each of B and C held together, work 2 rows with one strand each of A and C held together; rep from * for Color Sequence.

NOTE: To change color, work last stitch until 2 loops remain on hook, yarn over with new color, and draw yarn through 2 loops on hook to complete stitch.

AFGHAN

With 1 strand each of A and B held together, ch 70.

Row 1: Dc in 4th ch from hook and each ch across – 67 dc.

Change to 1 strand each of B and C held tog.

Rows 2-3: Ch 3 (does not count as st), dc in each dc across.

Change to 1 strand each of A and C held together.

Rep Row 2 and continue in Color Sequence for a total of 35 rows.

Change to 1 strand each of A and B held together.

Last Row: Rep Row 2. Do not fasten off.

FINISHING
Edging
From right side with 1 strand each of A and B held tog.

Rnd 1: Ch 1, turn, work 3 sc in first dc, sc in each dc across, work 3 sc in last dc; turn to work along side edge, sc evenly spaced along side, work 3 sc in corner; turn to work in free loops along opposite edge of foundation ch, sc in each ch across, work 3 sc in last ch; turn to work along opposite side, sc evenly spaced along side; join with sl st in first sc.

Rnd 2: Ch 1, turn, sc in each sc around, working 3 sc in each corner; join with sl st in first sc.

Rnd 3: Ch 1, turn, *sl st in next sc, ch 2, sl st in 2nd ch from hook (picot made), skip 1 sc, sl st in next sc; rep from * around; join with sl st in beg ch.

Fasten off. Weave in ends.

pattern stitchSQUARES

Now that you've seen some amazing projects made from one simple block or a single pattern stitch, we're giving you 13 additional pattern stitches. (Don't forget the Multi-Color Granny Square on pages 18 & 19.) We crocheted each pattern stitch into a 10" square, then used computer generation to duplicate the squares into a variety of imaginary throws (pages 52-57). Let these possibilities inspire you to create your own afghans from the squares. For an edging, a reverse single crochet stitch works well on graphic afghans like these. Learning to improvise and create your own designs is truly rewarding. And you know the Vanna's Choice yarn colors will make your creations look lovely!

half double crochet
STRIPED SQUARE

■□□□ BEGINNER

Finished Size: 10" x 10" (25.5 x 25.5 cm)

MATERIALS
LION BRAND® Vanna's Choice Worsted Weight
   yarn [3.5 ounces, 170 yards
   (100 grams, 156 meters) per ball]
   1 ball #105 Silver Blue (A)
   1 ball #108 Dusty Blue (B)
   (makes 4 squares)
   or colors of your choice
   LION BRAND Size K-10.5 [6.5 mm] crochet hook
   or size needed for gauge
LION BRAND large-eyed blunt needle

MEDIUM 4

GAUGE
11 half double crochet and 8 rows = 4" [10 cm]
BE SURE TO CHECK YOUR GAUGE.

NOTE: To change color work last stitch of first color until 3 loops remain on hook, yarn over with next color, draw yarn through all loops on hook to complete stitch.

SQUARE
With A, chain 28.
Row 1: Half double crochet in 3rd chain from hook and in each chain across –- 26 half double crochet.
Row 2: Chain 2, turn, half double crochet in each half double crochet across; change to B in last stitch.
Rows 3 and 4: Chain 2, turn, half double crochet in each half double crochet across; change to A in last stitch of Row 4.
Rows 5 and 6: Chain 2, turn, half double crochet in each half double crochet across; change to B in last stitch of Row 4.
Rows 7 and 8: Chain 2, turn, half double crochet in each half double crochet across; change to B in last stitch of Row 4.
Repeat Rows 5-8 three more times (for a total of 20 rows). Fasten off.

FINISHING
Weave in ends.

spike clusterSQUARE

□■□□ EASY

Finished Size: 10" x 10" (25.5 x 25.5 cm)

MATERIALS
LION BRAND® Vanna's Choice Worsted Weight
   yarn [3.5 ounces, 170 yards
   (100 grams, 156 meters) per ball]
   1 ball #101 Pink (A)
   1 ball #173 Dusty Green (B)
   (makes 4 squares)
   or colors of your choice
LION BRAND Size K-10.5 [6.5 mm] crochet hook
   or size needed for gauge
LION BRAND large-eyed blunt needle

GAUGE
9½ sts and 13 rows = 4" [10 cm]
BE SURE TO CHECK YOUR GAUGE.

NOTE: To change color work last stitch of first
color until 2 loops remain on hook, yarn over with
next color, draw yarn through 2 loops on hook to
complete stitch.

STITCH EXPLANATION
SPC (Spike Cluster): Over same st pick up 5 spike
loops by inserting hook as follows:
2 sts to right and 1 row below next st; 1 st to right and
2 rows below; 3 rows directly below same st; 1 st to
left and 2 rows below; 2 sts to left and 1 row below,
then draw up a loop in same st – 7 loops on hook.
Yarn over and draw through all loops.

SQUARE
With A, chain 25.
Row 1: Sc in 2nd ch from hook and each ch across –- 24 sc.
Rows 2-4: Ch 1, turn, sc in each sc across; change to B in last st of Row 4.
Row 5: Ch 1, turn, sc in next 3 sc, (SPC over next st, sc in next 7 sc) twice, SPC over next st, sc in last 4 sc.
Rows 6-8: Work as for Row 2; change to A in last st of Row 8.
Row 9: Ch 1, turn, sc in next 7 sc, SPC over next st, sc in next 7 sc, SPC over next st, sc in last 8 sc.
Rows 10-12: Ch 1, turn, sc in each sc across; change to B in last st of Row 12.
Rows 13-28: Repeat Rows 5-12 twice.
Rows 29-32: Repeat Rows 5-8.
Fasten off.

FINISHING
Weave in ends.

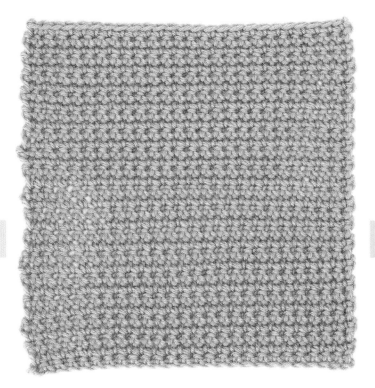

single crochet
SQUARE

⬤▢▢▢ **BEGINNER**

Finished Size: 10" x 10" (25.5 x 25.5 cm)

MATERIALS

LION BRAND® Vanna's Choice Worsted Weight
  yarn [3.5 ounces, 170 yards
  (100 grams, 156 meters) per ball]
  1 ball makes 2 squares
LION BRAND Size K-10.5 [6.5 mm] crochet hook
  or size needed for gauge
LION BRAND large-eyed blunt needle

MEDIUM 4

GAUGE

10 single crochet and 14 rows = 4" [10 cm]
BE SURE TO CHECK YOUR GAUGE.

SQUARE

Chain 26.
Row 1: Single crochet in 2nd chain from hook and
in each chain across –- 25 single crochet.
Rows 2-34: Chain 1, turn, single crochet in each
single crochet across.
Fasten off.

FINISHING

Weave in ends.

half double crochet
SQUARE

Finished Size: 10" x 10" (25.5 x 25.5 cm)

MATERIALS

LION BRAND® Vanna's Choice Worsted Weight
yarn [3.5 ounces, 170 yards
(100 grams, 156 meters) per ball]
1 ball makes 2½ squares
LION BRAND Size K-10.5 [6.5 mm] crochet hook
or size needed for gauge
LION BRAND large-eyed blunt needle

GAUGE

11 half double crochet and 8 rows = 4" [10 cm]
BE SURE TO CHECK YOUR GAUGE.

SQUARE

Chain 28.
Row 1: Half double crochet in 3rd chain from hook and
in each chain across – 26 half double crochet.
Rows 2-20: Chain 2, turn, half double crochet in each
half double crochet across.
Fasten off.

FINISHING

Weave in ends.

double crochet
SQUARE

◼☐☐☐ BEGINNER

Finished Size: 10" x 10" (25.5 x 25.5 cm)

MATERIALS

LION BRAND® Vanna's Choice Worsted Weight
yarn [3.5 ounces, 170 yards
(100 grams, 156 meters) per ball]
1 ball makes 2 squares
LION BRAND Size K-10.5 [6.5 mm] crochet hook
or size needed for gauge
LION BRAND large-eyed blunt needle

GAUGE

11 double crochet and 6 rows = 4" [10 cm]
BE SURE TO CHECK YOUR GAUGE

SQUARE

Chain 28.
Row 1: Double crochet in 4th chain from hook and
in each chain across – 25 double crochet.
Rows 2-20: Chain 2, turn, double crochet in each
double crochet across.
Fasten off.

FINISHING

Weave in ends.

43

● ■ ☐ ☐ **EASY**

Finished Size: 10" x 10" (25.5 x 25.5 cm)

MATERIALS
LION BRAND® Vanna's Choice Worsted Weight
yarn [3.5 ounces, 170 yards
(100 grams, 156 meters) per ball]
1 ball

MEDIUM 4

LION BRAND Size J-10 [6 mm] crochet hook or
size needed for gauge
LION BRAND large-eyed blunt needle

GAUGE
12½ sc = 4" [10 cm]
BE SURE TO CHECK YOUR GAUGE.

SQUARE
Ch 32.

Row 1: Sc in 2nd ch from hook and each ch across
– 31 sc.

Row 2: Ch 1, turn, sc in first sc, *ch 1, sk next sc, sc
in next sc; rep from * across.

Row 3: Ch 1, turn, sc in first sc, *dc in next ch-1 sp,
sc in next sc; rep from * across.

Row 4: Ch 1, turn, sc in first sc, *ch 1, sk next dc, sc
in next sc; rep from * to end.

Rep Rows 3 and 4 until piece measures 9³/₄". [25
cm] from beginning, ending with Row 4.

Last Row: Ch 1, turn, sc in each sc and ch across.
Fasten off.

FINISHING
Weave in ends.

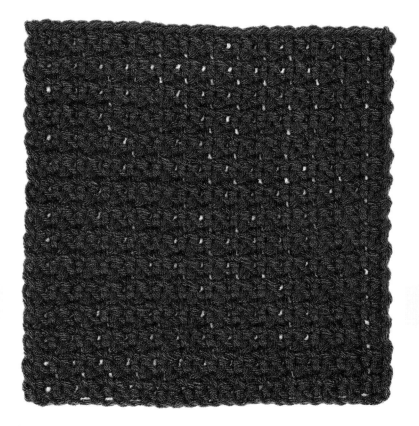

grit stitch
SQUARE

Finished Size: 10" x 10" (25.5 x 25.5 cm)

MATERIALS
LION BRAND® Vanna's Choice
  Worsted Weight yarn
  [3.5 ounces, 170 yards
  (100 grams, 156 meters) per ball]
  1 ball makes 2 squares
LION BRAND Size K-10.5 [6.5 mm]
  crochet hook or size needed
  for gauge
LION BRAND large-eyed blunt needle

GAUGE
12 single crochet and 12 rows = 4" [10 cm]
BE SURE TO CHECK YOUR GAUGE

SQUARE
Chain 32.
Row 1: Single crochet in 2nd chain from hook, *skip 1 chain, 2 single crochet in next chain; repeat from * to last 2 chain, skip 1 chain, single crochet in last chain – 30 single crochet.
Rows 2-20: Chain 1, turn, single crochet in first single crochet, *skip 1 single crochet, 2 single crochet in next single crochet; repeat from * to last single crochet, skip last single crochet, single crochet in top of turning chain.
Fasten off.

FINISHING
Weave in ends.

grannySQUARE

 EASY

Finished Size: 10" x 10" (25.5 x 25.5 cm)

MATERIALS
LION BRAND® Vanna's Choice
  Worsted Weight yarn
  [3.5 ounces, 170 yards
  (100 grams, 156 meters)
  per ball]
  1 ball
LION BRAND Size J-10 [6 mm]
  crochet hook or size needed
  for gauge
LION BRAND large-eyed blunt
  needle

GAUGE
3 rounds = 4¹/₂" [11.5 cm]
BE SURE TO CHECK YOUR GAUGE.

SQUARE
Ch 4; join with sl st in first ch to form
a ring.
Rnd 1: Ch 6 (counts as dc, ch 3 here
and throughout), [3 dc in ring, ch 3]
3 times, 2 dc in ring; join with sl st in
3rd ch of beg ch-6.
Rnd 2: Sl st into next ch-3 sp, ch 6,
3 dc in same ch-3 sp, ch 1, *(3 dc, ch 3,
3 dc) in next ch-3 sp, ch 1; rep from *
twice more, 2 dc in same sp as beg ch-6;
join with sl st in 3rd ch of beg ch-6.

Rnd 3: Sl st into next ch-3 sp, ch
6, 3 dc in same ch-3 sp, ch 1, 3 dc
in next ch-1 sp, ch 1, *(3 dc, ch 3,
3 dc) in next ch-3 sp, ch 1, 3 dc in
next ch-1 sp, ch 1; rep from * twice
more, 2 dc in same sp as beg ch-6;
join with sl st in 3rd ch of beg ch-6.
Rnd 4: Sl st into next ch-3 sp, ch
6, 3 dc in same ch-3 sp, (ch 1, 3 dc
in next ch-1 sp) twice, ch 1, *(3 dc,
ch 3, 3 dc) in next ch-3 sp, (ch 1, 3
dc in next ch-1 sp) twice, ch 1; rep
from * twice more, 2 dc in same sp
as beg ch-6; join with sl st in 3rd ch
of beg ch-6.
Rnd 5: Sl st into next ch-3 sp, ch 6,
3 dc in same ch-3 sp, (ch 1, 3 dc in
next ch-1 sp) 3 times, ch 1, *(3 dc,
ch 3, 3 dc) in next ch-3 sp, (ch 1,
3 dc in next ch-1 sp) 3 times, ch 1;
rep from * twice more, 2 dc in same
sp as beg ch-6; join with sl st in 3rd
ch of beg ch-6.

Rnd 6: Sl st into next ch-3 sp, ch 6,
3 dc in same ch-3 sp, (ch 1, 3 dc in
next ch-1 sp) 4 times, ch 1, *(3 dc,
ch 3, 3 dc) in next ch-3 sp, (ch 1, 3
dc in next ch-1 sp) 4 times, ch 1; rep
from * twice more, 2 dc in same sp
as beg ch-6; join with sl st in 3rd ch
of beg ch-6.
Rnd 7: Sl st into next ch-3 sp, ch 6,
3 dc in same ch-3 sp, (ch 1, 3 dc in
next ch-1 sp) 5 times, ch 1, *(3 dc,
ch 3, 3 dc) in next ch-3 sp, (ch 1, 3
dc in next ch-1 sp) 5 times, ch 1; rep
from * twice more, 2 dc in same sp a
beg ch-6; join with sl st in 3rd ch of
beg ch-6.
Fasten off.

FINISHING
Weave in ends.

eyelet laceSQUARE

■■□□ **EASY**

Finished Size: 10" x 10" (25.5 x 25.5 cm)

MATERIALS

LION BRAND® Vanna's Choice Worsted Weight
yarn [3.5 ounces, 170 yards
(100 grams, 156 meters) per ball]
1 ball
LION BRAND Size J-10 [6 mm] crochet hook or
size needed for gauge
LION BRAND large-eyed blunt needle

GAUGE

12 dc and 5½ rows = 4" [10 cm]
BE SURE TO CHECK YOUR GAUGE.

SQUARE

Ch 32.

Row 1: Dc in 4th ch from hook and each ch across.
Row 2: Ch 3 (counts as dc here and throughout), turn,
dc in next 2 dc, *ch 2, sk next 2 dc, dc in next 6 dc; rep
from * twice more, ch 2, sk 2 dc, dc in top of turning ch.

Row 3: Ch 3, turn, *dc in next 2 ch, dc in next 4 dc, ch
2, sk next 2 dc; rep from * twice more, dc in next 2 ch,
dc in next 2 dc, dc in top of turning ch.
Row 4: Ch 3, turn, *dc in next 4 dc, dc in next 2 ch, ch
2, sk next 2 dc; rep from * twice more, dc in next 4 dc,
dc in top of turning ch.
Row 5: Ch 3, turn, dc in next 2 dc, *ch 2, sk next 2 dc,
dc in next 2 ch, dc in next 4 dc; rep from * twice more,
ch 2, sk next 2 dc, dc in top of turning ch.
Row 6: Ch 3, turn, dc in next 2 ch, *ch 2, sk next 2 dc,
dc in next 4 dc, dc in next 2 ch; rep from * twice more,
ch 2, dc in top of turning ch.
Rows 7-10: Rep Rows 3-6.
Rows 11-13: Rep Rows 3-5.
Row 14: Ch 3, turn, dc in each dc and ch across – 30 dc.
Fasten off.

FINISHING

Weave in ends.

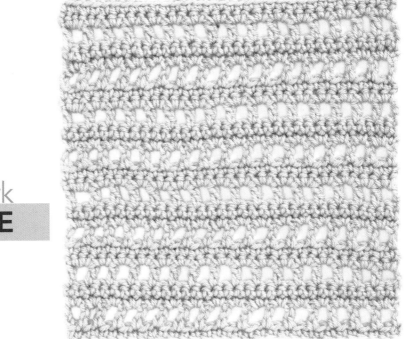

openwork
SQUARE

 EASY

Finished Size: 10" x 10" (25.5 x 25.5 cm)

MATERIALS

LION BRAND® Vanna's Choice Worsted Weight
   yarn [3.5 ounces, 170 yards
   (100 grams, 156 meters) per ball]
   1 ball

LION BRAND Size J-10 [6 mm] crochet hook or
   size needed for gauge

LION BRAND large-eyed blunt needle

GAUGE

13 sc = 4" [10 cm]
BE SURE TO CHECK YOUR GAUGE.

SQUARE

Ch 34.

Row 1: Sc in 2nd ch from hook and each ch
across – 33 sc.

Row 2: Ch 4 (counts as dc, ch 1), turn, sk
first 2 sc, dc in next sc, *ch 1, sk next sc, dc in
next sc; rep from * across.

Row 3: Ch 1, turn, sc in first dc, 2 sc in each
ch-sp across, ending with 2 sc in ch-1 sp of
turning ch.

Row 4: Ch 1, turn, sc in each sc across.

Rep Rows 2-4 until Square measures 10" [25.5
cm] from beginning, ending with Row 4.
Fasten off.

FINISHING

Weave in ends.

criss cross SQUARE

■■□□ EASY

Finished Size: 10" x 10 (25.5 x 25.5 cm)

MATERIALS
LION BRAND® Vanna's Choice Worsted Weight yarn [3.5 ounces, 170 yards (100 grams, 156 meters) per ball] MEDIUM 4
1 ball
LION BRAND Size J-10 [6 mm] crochet hook or size needed for gauge
LION BRAND large-eyed blunt needle

GAUGE
3 rounds = 4½" [11.5 cm]
BE SURE TO CHECK YOUR GAUGE.

SQUARE
Ch 6; join with sl st in first ch to form a ring.

Rnd 1: Ch 3 (counts as dc here and throughout), 3 dc in ring, ch 3, (4 dc in ring, ch 3) 3 times; join with sl st in top of beg ch-3.

Rnd 2: Ch 3, sk next 2 dc, dc in next dc, (2 dc, ch 3, 2 dc) in next ch-3 sp, *dc in next dc, sk next 2 dc, dc in next dc, (2 dc, ch 3, 2 dc) in next ch-3 sp; rep from * twice more; join with sl st in 3rd ch of beg ch-3.

Rnd 3: Ch 5 (counts as dc, ch 2 here and throughout), dc in next 3 dc, (2 dc, ch 3, 2 dc) in next ch-3 sp, *dc in next 3 dc, ch 2, dc in next 3 dc, (2 dc, ch 3, 2 dc) in next ch-3 sp; rep from * twice more, dc in next 2 dc; join with sl st in 3rd ch of beg ch-5.

Rnd 4: Ch 5, dc in next 5 dc, (2 dc, ch 3, 2 dc) in next ch-3 sp, *dc in next 5 dc, ch 2, dc in next 5 dc, (2 dc, ch 3, 2 dc) in next ch-3 sp; rep from * twice more, dc in next 4 dc; join with sl st in 3rd ch of beg ch-5.

Rnd 5: Ch 5, dc in next 7 dc, (2 dc, ch 3, 2 dc) in next ch-3 sp, *dc in next 7 dc, ch 2, dc in next 7 dc, (2 dc, ch 3, 2 dc) in next ch-3 sp; rep from * twice more, dc in next 6 dc; join with sl st in 3rd ch of beg ch-5.

Rnd 6: Ch 5, dc in next 9 dc, (2 dc, ch 3, 2 dc) in next ch-3 sp, *dc in next 9 dc, ch 2, dc in next 9 dc, (2 dc, ch 3, 2 dc) in next ch-3 sp; rep from * twice more, dc in next 8 dc; join with sl st in 3rd ch of beg ch-5.

Rnd 7: Ch 1, sc in same st, 2 sc in next ch-2 sp, sc in next 11 dc, (2 sc, ch 3, 2 sc) in next ch-3 sp, *sc in next 11 dc, 2 sc in next ch-2 sp, sc in next 11 dc, (2 sc, ch 3, 2 sc) in next ch-3 sp; rep from * twice more, sc in next 10 dc; join with sl st in first sc. Fasten off.

FINISHING
Weave in ends.

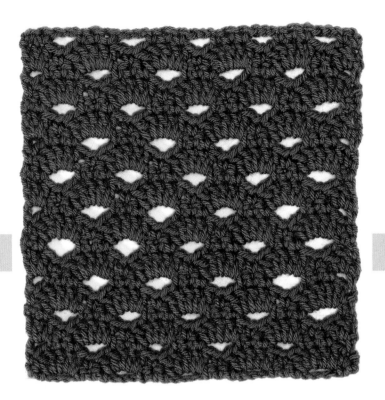

shell lace
SQUARE

Finished Size: 10" x 10" (25.5 x 25.5 cm)

MATERIALS

LION BRAND® Vanna's Choice Worsted Weight
yarn [3.5 ounces, 170 yards
(100 grams, 156 meters) per ball]
1 ball

LION BRAND Size J-10 [6 mm] crochet hook or
size needed for gauge

LION BRAND large-eyed blunt needle

GAUGE

12½ dc = 4" [10 cm]
BE SURE TO CHECK YOUR GAUGE.

SQUARE

Ch 32.

Row 1: Sc in 2nd ch from hook, sc in next ch, *ch 3, sk 3 ch, sc in next 3 ch; rep from * to last 5 ch, ch 3, sk 3 ch, sc in last 2 ch.

Row 2: Ch 1, turn, sc in first sc, *5 dc in next ch-3 sp, sk 1 sc, sc in next sc; rep from * across.

Row 3: Ch 3, turn, sk first dc, sc in next 3 dc, *ch 3, sk next 2 dc, sc in next 3 dc; rep from * across, ch 2, sc in last sc.

Row 4: Ch 3, turn, 2 dc in next ch-2 sp, sk next sc, sc in next sc, *5 dc in next ch-3 sp, sk next sc, sc in next sc; rep from * across, 3 dc in last ch-3 sp.

Row 5: Ch 1, turn, sc in first 2 dc, ch 3, sk next 2 dc, *sc in next 3 dc, ch 3, sk next 2 dc; rep from * across, sc in next dc, sc in top of turning ch.

Rep Rows 2-5 until Square measures 10" [25.5 cm] from beginning, ending with Row 5. Fasten off.

FINISHING

Weave in ends.

◼◼◻◻ **EASY**

Finished Size: 10" x 10"
(25.5 x 25.5 cm)

MATERIALS
LION BRAND® Vanna's Choice
Worsted Weight yarn
[3.5 ounces, 170 yards **MEDIUM 4**
(100 grams, 156 meters)
per ball]
1 ball
LION BRAND Size J-10 [6 mm]
crochet hook or size needed
for gauge
LION BRAND large-eyed blunt
needle

GAUGE
12$\frac{1}{2}$ dc and 6$\frac{1}{2}$ rows = 4" [10 cm]
BE SURE TO CHECK YOUR
GAUGE.

SQUARE
Ch 33.
Row 1: Dc in 4th ch from hook and
each ch across.
Row 2: Ch 3 (counts as dc here and
throughout), turn, dc in each dc
across, dc in top of turning ch –
31 dc.
Row 3: Ch 3, turn, dc in next 4 dc,
*ch 4, (sk 1 dc, tr in next dc) 4 times,
ch 4, sk 1 dc, dc in next 3 dc; rep
from * once, dc in next dc, dc in top
of turning ch.
Row 4: Ch 3, turn, dc in next 4 dc,
*ch 4, sc in next 4 tr, ch 4, dc in next
3 dc; rep from * once, dc in next dc,
dc in top of turning ch.
Row 5: Ch 3, turn, dc in next 4 dc,
*ch 4, sc in next 4 sc, ch 4, dc in next
3 dc; rep from * once, dc in next dc,
dc in top of turning ch.

Row 6: Ch 3, turn, dc in next 4 dc,
*(ch 1, tr in next sc) 4 times, ch 1, dc
in next 3 dc; rep from * once, dc in
next dc, dc in top of turning ch.
Row 7: Ch 3, turn, dc in next 4 dc,
*(dc in next ch-1 sp, dc in next tr)
4 times, dc in next ch-1 sp, dc in
next 3 dc; rep from * once, dc in next
dc, dc in top of turning ch.
Rows 8 and 9: Rep Row 2.
Rows 10-16: Rep Rows 3-9.
Fasten off.

FINISHING
Weave in ends.

afghanOPTIONS

Let these possibilities inspire you to create your own afghans from the pattern stitch squares.

optionONE

Multi-Color Granny Squares: Chocolate, #126; Honey, #130; Brick, #133; Rust, #135

Inner Accent Squares: Chocolate, #126, Tiny Textures Square

Main Color Squares: Honey, #135, Tiny Texture Square

Center: Black, #153, Webbed Lace Square

Inner Border: Honey, #130, Tiny Textures Square

Middle Border: Beige, #123, Criss Cross Square

Outer Border: Chocolate, #126, Tiny Textures Square

optionTWO

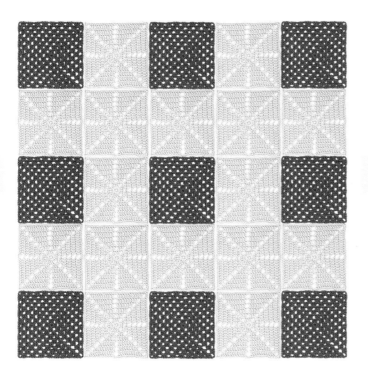

optionTHREE

Main Color Squares: Beige, #123, Criss Cross Square

Accent Color Squares: Taupe, #125, Solid Granny Square

optionFOUR

Rows 1 and 4: Chocolate, #126, Tiny Texture Square; Honey, #130, Tiny Textures Square

Rows 2 and 5: Pea Green, #170, Single Crochet Square; Mustard, #158, Half Double Crochet Square

Rows 3 and 6: Colonial Blue, #109, Grit Stitch Square; Dusty Blue, #108, Half Double Crochet Square

optionFIVE

Center Squares: Dusty Green, #173, Spike Cluster Square

Border Multi-Color Granny Squares: Olive, #174; Pea Green, #170; Dusty Green, #173; Linen, #099

Border Squares: Olive, #174, Criss Cross Square

Top Row: Brick, #133, Double Crochet Square; Pea Green, #170, Single Crochet Square; Mustard, #158, Half Double Crochet Square; Rust, #135, Eyelet Lace Square

optionSIX

optionSEVEN

Main Color Squares: Black, #153, Webbed Lace Square

Accent Color Squares: Linen, #099, Openwork Square

optionEIGHT

Row 1: Colonial Blue, #109, Grit Stitch Square; Mustard, #158, Half Double Crochet Square; Brick, #133, Double Crochet Square; Silver Blue, #105, Half Double Crochet Square; Pea Green, #170, Single Crochet Square

Row 2: Rust, #135, Eyelet Lace Square; Chocolate, #126, Tiny Textures Square; Dusty Blue, #108, Half Double Crochet Square; Mustard, #158, Half Double Crochet Square; Brick, #133, Double Crochet Square

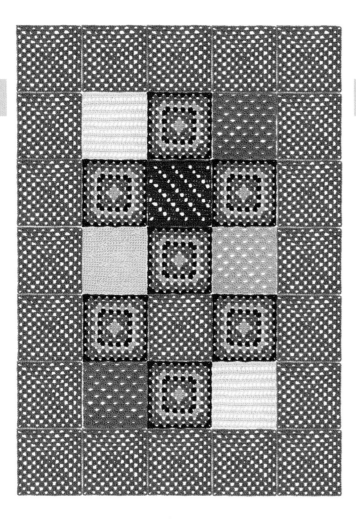

optionNINE

Center Squares: Linen, #099, Openwork Square; Purple #147, Rose #142, Dusty Purple #146, Dusty Rose #102 Multi-Color Granny Square; Dusty Purple #146, Shell Lace Square; Purple #147, Eyelet Lace Square; Pink #101, Spike Cluster Square; Dusty Rose #140, Shell Lace Square: Rose, #142, Solid Granny Square

Outer Border Squares: Rose, #142, Solid Granny Square

Center Squares: Silver Blue, #105, Half Double Crochet Square

Inner Border: Dusty Blue, #108, Half Double Crochet Square

Outer Border Squares: Dusty Blue, #108 and Silver Blue, #105, Striped Half Double Crochet Square

optionTEN

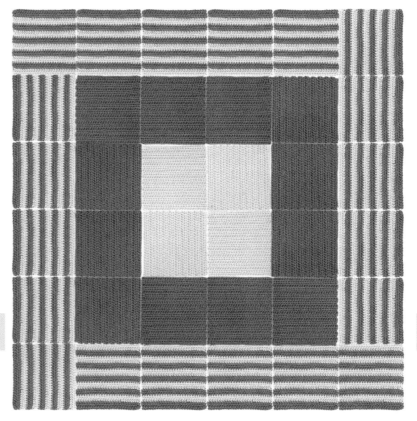

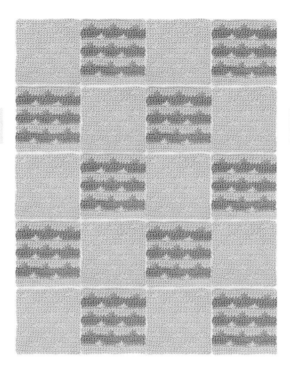

optionELEVEN

Solid Squares: Pink, #101, Spike Cluster Square

Striped Squares: Pink, #101 and Dusty Green, #173 Spike Cluster Square

optionTWELVE

Center Squares: Taupe, #125, Solid Granny Square

Inner Border: Dusty Rose, #140, Shell Lace Square

Outer Border: Linen, #099, Openwork Square

WARM UP AMERICA!

Since 1991, Warm Up America! has donated more than 250,000 afghans to battered women's shelters, victims of natural disaster, the homeless, and many others who are in need. As a new member of this organization's board of directors, I'm excited to share this afghan pattern with you.

You can help Warm Up America! help others, and with so little effort. Get your friends and family involved in knitting or crocheting 7" x 9" blocks that can be joined together into warm blankets and donated to a local charity or social services agency. Your heart will be warmed by the knowledge that you've helped someone in your community. Visit www.warmupamerica.org to find instructions for completing afghans, as well as a link where you can notify the organization of the afghans you distribute locally.

Remember, just a **little** bit of yarn can make **big** difference to someone in need!

warm up
AMERICA!
afghan

◖◼☐◻◻ EASY

Finished Size: 49" x 63" (124.5 x 160 cm) not including border

MATERIALS
LION BRAND® Vanna's Choice Worsted Weight yarn [3½ ounces, 170 yards (100 grams, 156 meters) per ball]
MEDIUM 4
1 ball #142 Rose (A)
1 ball #108 Dusty Blue (B)
2 balls #146 Dusty Purple (C)
1 ball #170 Pea Green (D)
1 ball #105 Silver Blue (E)
1 ball #173 Dusty Green (F)
1 ball #135 Rust (G)
1 ball #109 Colonial Blue (H)
2 balls #123 Beige (J)
2 balls #125 Taupe (K)
1 ball #101 Pink (L)
1 ball #143 Antique Rose (M)
1 ball #147 Purple (N)
1 ball #130 Honey (O)
1 ball #126 Chocolate (P)
1 ball #099 Linen (Q)
1 ball #133 Brick (R)
1 ball #158 Mustard (S)
1 ball #174 Olive (T)
1 ball #140 Dusty Rose (U)
1 ball #110 Navy (V)
or colors of your choice
LION BRAND Size I-9 [5.5 mm] crochet hook or size needed for gauge
LION BRAND large-eyed blunt needle

GAUGE
Block = 7" x 9" [18 x 23 cm]
BE SURE TO CHECK YOUR GAUGE.

NOTE: To change color work last stitch of first color to last yarn over, yarn over with next color and draw through loops on hook to complete stitch.

AFGHAN
STRIPED BLOCK
With D, ch 23.

Row 1: Dc in 4th ch from hook and in each ch across.

Rows 2-7: Ch 3 (counts as first dc), turn, dc in each dc across; change to C in last st of last row.

Row 8: Rep Row 2; change to B in last st.

Rows 9-11: Rep Row 2; change to A in last st of last row.

Rows 12-16: Rep Row 2.

Fasten off.

This completes Striped Block at upper left hand corner of chart.

Make 24 more Striped Blocks, working as for first Striped Block and following color sequences as shown on chart, working 7 rows in the first color, 1 row in the next color, 3 rows in the next color, and 5 rows in the last color.

SHELL BLOCK (Make 1 each with A, B, C, E, G, J, L, N, P, R, T and V)

Ch 25.

Row 1: 2 dc in 4th ch from hook (half shell made), sk 2 ch, *sc in next ch, sk 2 ch, 5 dc in next ch (shell made), sk 2 ch; rep from * to last ch, sc in last ch – 3½ shells.

Rows 2-16: Ch 3 (counts as first dc), turn, 2 dc in first sc, *sk next 2 dc, sc in next dc (center dc of shell), sk next 2 dc, shell in next sc; rep from * to last 3 dc, sk next 2 dc, sc in top of turning ch.

Row 17: Ch 3, turn, *hdc in next dc, sc in next 3 dc, hdc in next dc, dc in sc; rep from * to last 3 dc, hdc in next dc, sc in next dc, sc in turning ch.

Fasten off.

TEXTURE BLOCK (Make 1 each with A, B, C, D, F, H, K, M, O, Q, S and U)

Ch 23.

Row 1: Dc in 4th ch form hook and in each ch across.

CHART

A B C D	A Shell	B C D E	B Texture	C D E F	C Shell	D E F G
D Texture	E F G H	E Shell	F G H J	F Texture	G H J K	G Shell
H J K L	H Texture	J K L M	J Shell	K L M N	K Texture	L M N O
L Shell	M N O P	M Texture	N O P Q	N Shell	O P Q R	O Texture
P Q R S	P Shell	Q R S T	Q Texture	R S T U	R Shell	S T U V
S Texture	T U V A	T Shell	U V A B	U Texture	V A B C	V Shell
A B C D	A Texture	B C D E	B Shell	C D E F	C Texture	D E F G

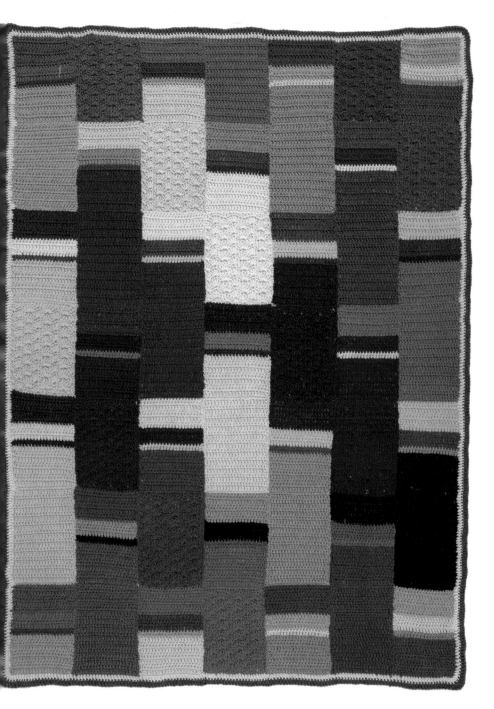

Row 2: Ch 1, turn, sc in first dc and each dc across, sc in top of turning ch.

Row 3: Ch 3 (counts as first dc), turn, dc in each sc across.

Rows 4-21: Rep Rows 2 and 3.

Fasten off.

FINISHING
Following chart for placement, sew Blocks together.

Edging
Rnd 1: Join J with sl st in any st along edge, ch 2, dc evenly around entire Afghan, working 3 dc in each corner; join with sl st in first dc. Fasten off.

Rnd 2: Join K with sl st in any st along edge, rep Rnd 1.

Fasten off. Weave in ends.

general INSTRUCTIONS

ABBREVIATIONS

beg = begin(s)(ning)
ch(s) = chain(s)
ch-sp = space previously made
cm = centimeters
dc = double crochet(s)
hdc = half double crochet(s)
mm = millimeters
rep = repeat
rnd(s) = round(s)
RS = right side
sc = single crochet(s)
sk = skip
sl = slip
sl st = slip stitch(es)
sp(s) = space(s)
st(s) = stitch(es)
tog = together
tr = treble crochet(s)
yo = yarn over hook

* — When you see an asterisk used within a pattern row, the symbol indicates that later you will be told to repeat a portion of the instruction. Most often the instructions will say, repeat from * so many times.

( ) or [ ] — Set off a short number of stitches that are repeated or indicate additional information.

GAUGE

Never underestimate the importance of gauge. Achieving the correct gauge assures that the finished size of your piece matches the finished size given in the pattern.

CHECKING YOUR GAUGE

Work a swatch that is at least 4" (10 cm) square. Use the suggested hook size and the number of stitches given. For example, the standard Lion Brand® Vanna's Choice gauge is: 12 single crochet + 15 rows = 4" (10 cm) on a size J-10 (6 mm) hook. If your swatch is larger than 4" (10 cm), you need to work it again using a smaller hook; if it is smaller than 4" (10 cm), try it with a larger hook. This might require a swatch or two to get the exact gauge given in the pattern.

METRICS

As a handy reference, keep in mind that 1 ounce = approximately 28 grams and 1" = 2.5 centimeters.

TERMS

continue in this way or as established — Once a pattern is set up (established), the instructions may tell you to continue in the same way.

fasten off — To end your piece, you need to simply pull the yarn through the last loop left on the hook. This keeps the last stitch intact and prevents the work from unraveling.

right side — Refers to the front of the piece.

work even — This is used to indicate an area worked as established without increasing or decreasing.

HINTS

As in all pieces, good finishing techniques make a big difference in the quality of the piece: Do not tie knots. Always start a new skein at the beginning of a row or round, leaving ends long enough to weave in later.

basic crochet STITCHES and TECHNIQUES

SLIP STITCH
(abbreviated sl st)
To work a slip stitch, insert hook in stitch indicated, yo and draw through st and through loop on hook (**Fig. 1**).

Fig. 1

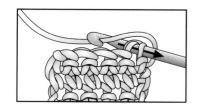

SINGLE CROCHET
(abbreviated sc)
Insert hook in stitch indicated, yo and pull up a loop, yo and draw through both loops on hook (**Fig. 2**).

Fig. 2

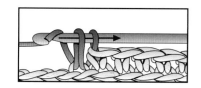

REVERSE SINGLE CROCHET
Working from left to right, * insert hook in st to right of hook (**Fig. 3a**), YO and draw through, under and to left of loop on hook (2 loops on hook) (**Fig. 3b**), YO and draw through both loops on hook (**Fig. 3c**) (reverse sc made, **Fig. 3d**); repeat from * around.

Fig. 3a

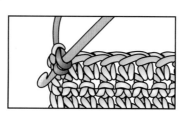

Fig. 3b

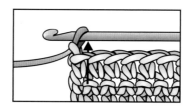

Fig. 3c

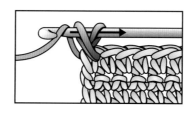

Fig. 3d

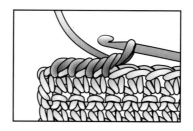

HALF DOUBLE CROCHET
(abbreviated hdc)
Yo, insert hook in stitch indicated, yo and pull up a loop, yo and draw through all 3 loops on hook (**Fig. 4**).

Fig. 4

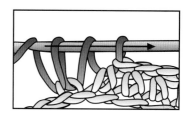

DOUBLE CROCHET
(abbreviated dc)
YO, insert hook in stitch indicated, yo and pull up a loop (3 loops on hook), yo and draw through 2 loops on hook (**Fig. 5a**), yo and draw through remaining 2 loops on hook (**Fig. 5b**).

Fig. 5a

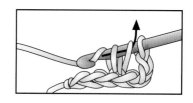

Fig. 5b

TREBLE CROCHET
(abbreviated tr)

YO twice, insert hook in stitch indicated, yo and pull up a loop (4 loops on hook) *(Fig. 6a)*, (yo and draw through 2 loops on hook) 3 times *(Fig. 6b)*.

Fig. 6a

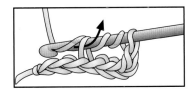

Fig. 6b

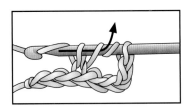

FRINGE

Cut a piece of cardboard 5" wide and ¹/₂" longer than you want your finished fringe to be. Wind the yarn **loosely** and **evenly** lengthwise around the cardboard until the card is filled, then cut across one end; repeat as needed.

Hold together half as many strands of yarn as desired for the finished fringe; fold in half.

With **wrong** side facing and using a crochet hook, draw the folded end up through the indicated stitch, space, or row and pull the loose ends through the folded end *(Fig. 7a)*; draw the knot up **tightly** *(Fig. 7b)*. Repeat, spacing as desired or as specified in instructions.

Lay flat on a hard surface and trim the ends.

Fig. 7a

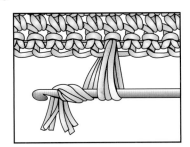

Fig. 7b

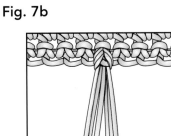

TASSEL

Cut a piece of cardboard 3" wide and as long as you want your finished tassel to be. Wind a double strand of yarn around the cardboard approximately 12 times. Cut an 18" length of yarn and insert it under all of the strands at the top of the cardboard; pull up **tightly** and tie securely. Leave the yarn ends long enough to attach the tassel. Cut the yarn at the opposite end of the cardboard and then remove it *(Fig. 8a)*. Cut a length of yarn and wrap it **tightly** around the tassel twice, 1" below the top *(Fig. 8b)*; tie securely. Trim the ends.

Fig. 8a

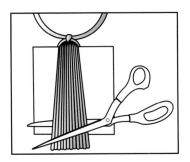

Fig. 8b

WHIPSTITCH

Place two squares with **wrong** sides together. Beginning in center of corner chs, sew through both pieces once to secure the beginning of the seam, leaving an ample yarn end to weave in later. Insert the needle from **front** to **back** through **both** loops on **both** pieces *(Fig. 9)*. Bring the needle around and insert it from **front** to **back** through next loops of both pieces. Continue in this manner to corner, keeping the sewing yarn fairly loose.

Fig. 9

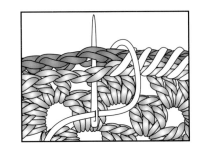

Lion Brand Yarn Company
34 West 15th Street
New York, New York 10011
www.LionBrand.com